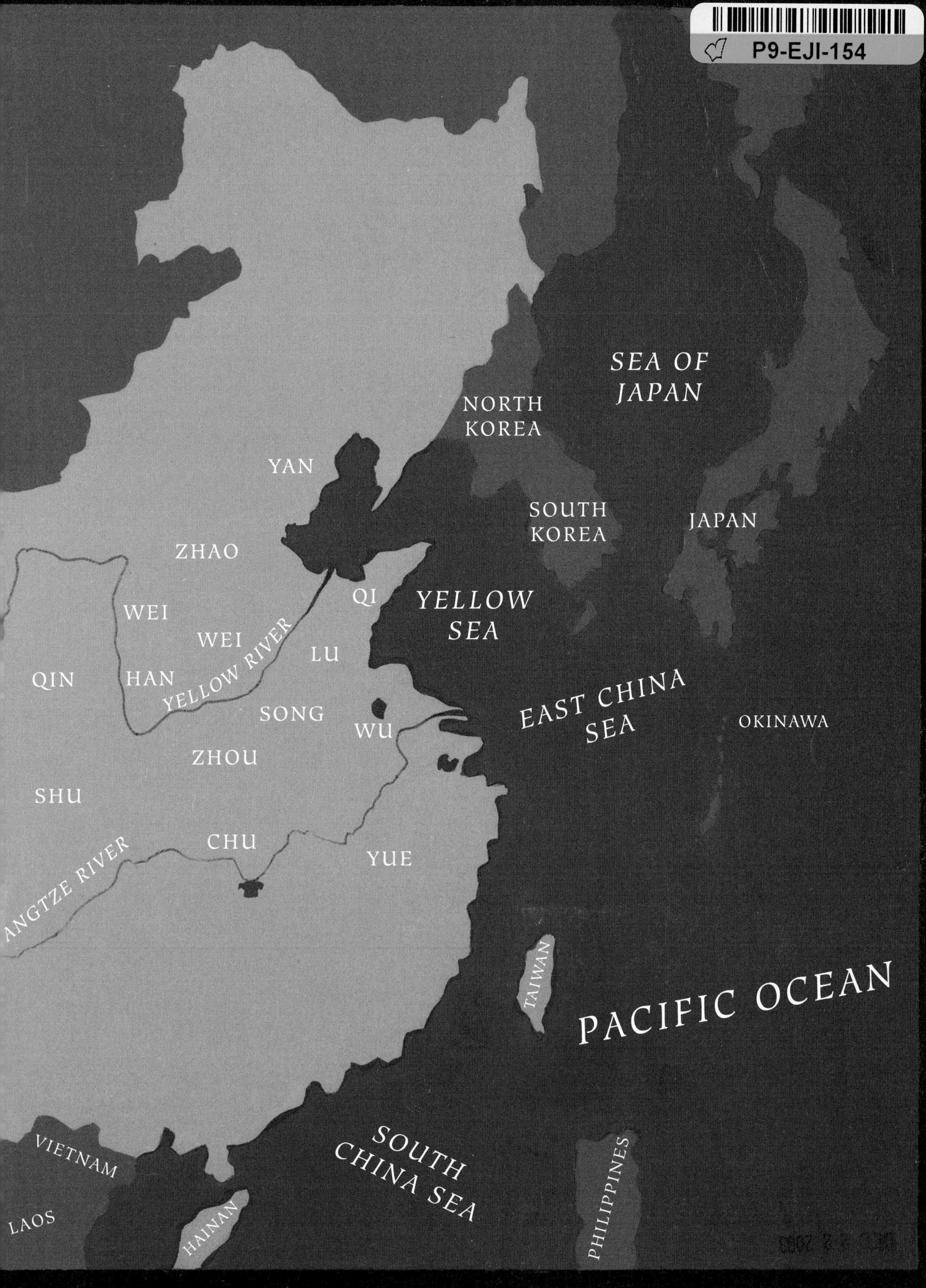
SEA OF JAPAN
NORTH KOREA
SOUTH KOREA
JAPAN
YAN
ZHAO
QI
YELLOW SEA
WEI
WEI
LU
QIN
HAN
YELLOW RIVER
SONG
WU
EAST CHINA SEA
OKINAWA
ZHOU
SHU
CHU
YUE
YANGTZE RIVER
TAIWAN
PACIFIC OCEAN
VIETNAM
SOUTH CHINA SEA
LAOS
HAINAN
PHILIPPINES

WEN CHANG, God of Literature

THE GODS AND GODDESSES OF ANCIENT CHINA

LEONARD EVERETT FISHER

Holiday House / New York

Humankind as the Universe

INTRODUCTION

China—its very name evokes mystery to the Western world. More than two thousand years ago, a king from Qin named Yin Zheng conquered and unified a group of independent states. The people of his new kingdom spoke and wrote different languages, wore different clothing, weighed and measured things differently, and used different monies. This unified state became China.

Yin Zheng, now called Qin Shi Huangdi, the First Supreme Emperor of China, did his best to standardize weights, measures, and money. He even ordered the people of his new empire to wear black clothes so that everyone would look alike. In modern times, Mao Zedong, the leader of the People's Republic of China, also made everyone wear the same clothing, but in blue.

Yet Qin Shi Huangdi was unable to standardize the many languages. Nor could he unify or simplify the widespread belief in countless gods who varied widely from region to region, even from person to person. The mythology of ancient China is crowded with gods and goddesses. These immortals reflected the rank and actions of human beings. Just as there were doctors on Earth, there were doctors among the gods, as well as emperors, empresses, kings, and queens. In fact, in Chinese mythology, many human beings who achieved renown in their earthly lives were transformed into gods and continued their activities in heaven. None of these gods were unified by rules and ceremonies that could pass for an organized religion. Instead, through the years, they were worshiped individually in addition to, or instead of, the more formal doctrines of Confucianism, Buddhism, Judaism, Islam, and Christianity.

A brief introduction to seventeen of the most popular of these gods and goddesses follows.

YU HUANG DA DI
The Jade Emperor

The god who stood at the top of all the immortal deities of ancient China—the most powerful and the most mysterious god, who was thought to have been a prince in ancient China—was Yu Huang Da Di, the Jade Emperor. No one was above him—his name even means "superior emperor." Yu Huang Da Di had the final word in all the affairs of heaven.

Yu Huang Da Di became the great organizer of the universe, straightening out much of the confusion in heaven. Once he created order out of chaos, he left ordinary affairs to lower gods and retired to enjoy a perfect immortal life. So he had little to do with human beings—they never worshiped or complained to him—and today remains a distant character.

Yu Huang Da Di was called the Jade Emperor because he was compared to jade, the most precious and perfect of all gemstones in ancient China.

NÜWA AND FUXI
Goddess of Humankind
God of Fire

Nüwa—part woman, part dragon—lived on Earth before there were people. She had a loving friendship with Fuxi, a male creature like herself—part man, part dragon. But Nüwa was still lonely and roamed the earth in search of more company. Finding none, Nüwa fashioned humanlike dolls from the mud of the great Yellow River. When she finished molding them, she blew her warm breath on them and they came to life. From that moment, people regarded Nüwa as their mother. But Nüwa did not plan on spending eternity creating men and women out of mud. She invented marriage so that human beings could people the earth without her help.

Fuxi was the world's first teacher; he taught human beings how to survive. He gave them fire and taught them how to use it. He also taught people how to make and use fishing nets. Once Fuxi gave people the basic knowledge of survival, he taught them how to create music. Finally, Fuxi invented written symbols to foretell the future—whether life was going to be better or worse; if sick people would recover or die; if a war would be won or lost; if there would be a feast or famine, drought or flood.

Nüwa and Fuxi were the first creatures to befriend the human race. They were thought to be the strongest protectors and most generous benefactors of the people of ancient China.

SUN WUKONG
God of Mischief

Sun is the Chinese word for "monkey," but Sun Wukong was no ordinary animal. To begin with, he was hatched from a stone egg. Later he became the king of a band of monkeys after leading them to a bountiful place atop a mountain, where they could enjoy their lives, eating and drinking all they ever wanted.

But Sun Wukong wanted more—he wanted to live forever. A holy man taught him how to somersault among the clouds, and transform into anything at all, and also gave him the secrets of immortality.

When Sun Wukong returned to his mountain paradise, he found that it had been invaded by a demon. He destroyed the demon with darts made from his own hair, a trick he learned from the holy man. Needing a better weapon, he asked for and received an iron pole from a sea dragon king. Sun Wukong demanded so many more things that the Jade Emperor arrested him and sent him to the underworld—to his death. There Sun Wukong quickly found his name and erased it. By doing that, he could never die. He was brought back to heaven, where he could be watched, and made Guardian of the Imperial Peach Garden. These peaches were the fruit of immortality. Instead of guarding them, Sun Wukong ate them all!

The Monkey King was such trouble that a metal band was placed on his head to keep him in line. Whenever Sun Wukong created some mischief, the band would tighten to remind him of his folly.

GUANYIN
Goddess of Mercy

Guanyin was originally a god in India named Avalokitesvara, which means "One Who Gazes Down upon the World and Hears the Cries of the People." A merciful god, Avalokitesvara was very popular among the people. Eventually, travelers, merchants, and religious missionaries from India introduced the god to China.

The Chinese liked the idea of a god who could hear their cries for mercy and rescue them from their difficult lives. They adopted Avalokitesvara as their own. However, over a long period of time, the Chinese made two changes. They changed the god's Indian name to Guanyin, which in Chinese has the same meaning. And since they viewed compassion as more female than male, the Indian male god became a Chinese female goddess.

Many Chinese people believed that Guanyin was really Miaoshan, a kind human princess who had been executed for not marrying the prince her father had chosen. When heaven's Jade Emperor learned of Miaoshan's death, he rescued her soul from the underworld. Then he brought her back to life by joining her soul to her body. Thereafter, Miaoshan was able to separate her soul from her body and see dangers that no one else could see. Once she saw the dangers—chiefly of sailors in trouble at sea—she was able to rescue those who were at risk.

ZHONG KUI
God of Healing

In ancient China the practice of medicine was already a highly developed craft, even though failure and death were more likely results than success and cure. Medicine men and surgeons were held in such honor that they enjoyed more respect than princes and kings.

Zhong Kui was an apprentice doctor. Centuries ago he studied hard and passed the required examinations, but he was never allowed to practice medicine. All his hard work had gone for nothing. The emperor would not permit him to work as a doctor and attend the sick and injured. Zhong Kui was so upset by this that, in his agony, he committed suicide right at the entrance to the palace.

Not long after that, the emperor dreamed that he was being attacked by a demon, but Zhong Kui drove it off and saved his life. As a result, the emperor made Zhong Kui a god, naming him the Great Spirit Healer of Demons in the Empire. Even his painted image is credited with frightening away demons or ghosts.

NIU LANG AND ZHI NÜ
God and Goddess of Love

Niu Lang, or Ox Boy, was the youngest of three brothers. After his parents died, his brothers divided their property among themselves, leaving Ox Boy with only a poor piece of land and an old ox. But this ox was special; he had once been a star but was made into an animal as a punishment for disobeying orders. Ox Boy worked hard on his poor land, but produced little.

One day, Ox Boy, on the advice of the ox, stole the clothes of Zhi Nü, the Goddess of Weaving, one of the seven beautiful star maidens who had descended from heaven to bathe in a nearby pool. Without her clothes, the star maiden could not return to heaven with her sisters. No matter. She fell in love with Ox Boy. They married and became the parents of a boy and a girl. Ox Boy had found happiness.

Meanwhile, heaven's gods and goddesses fumed over the marriage. Ox Boy was not good enough for a goddess.

Finally warriors were sent to drag the Goddess of Weaving back to heaven. Ox Boy tried to follow with their children, but the Jade Emperor drew a line across the sky that was so wide that Ox Boy and his children could not cross it. This river of stars became the Milky Way. However, the gods took pity on the couple and allowed Ox Boy and the Goddess of Weaving to visit each other on the seventh night of the seventh month of each year.

The Goddess of Weaving can be seen on one side of the Milky Way as Vega, the brightest star in the constellation Lyra. Ox Boy shines opposite as the star Altair in the constellation Aquila.

GUAN GONG
God of War

Guan Gong—Lord Guan—once called Guan Yu and later known as Guan Di—Emperor Guan—was a famous and well-liked soldier before he became a god.

After the first emperor of China, Qin Shi Huangdi, died in c. 210 B.C.E., the states he had welded into one country began to squabble with one another. Centuries later, out of the turmoil emerged three separate countries: Wei, Wu, and Shu. Guan Gong led the army of King Liu Bei of Shu.

Guan Gong was an unbeatable warrior and a loyal, generous man who always did what was right. He used his immense strength to help the weak and disadvantaged.

One story told how Guan Gong rescued a young girl kidnapped by the son of a local chieftain. Guan Gong killed the kidnapper, returned the girl to her distraught father, and then fled for his life, pursued by the chieftain's men. They chased him into a temple and set it on fire. Guan Gong came roaring out of the burning building, his face red from the flames, and slew every one of his pursuers.

Years later, Guan Gong was captured and executed for refusing to betray his king. After his death he was worshiped as a strong, righteous man. Temples were erected to his spirit throughout China so that people could ask him to protect them from demons, thieves, and scoundrels. Gradually Guan Gong became Guan Di—the emperor god, a god of the highest order. He was revered both as the patron of the military, but also of scholars, since he would recite great tracts of Chinese literature from memory.

XI WANG MU
Goddess of Immortality

Xi Wang Mu, Queen Mother of the West, was no beauty. In fact, she was something of a hag, and just as fearsome. Her tangled hair hung on her misshapen body like worn rope. Her teeth were those of a tiger, sharp and menacing. She even sported a tail—a leopard's tail. She would send plagues to human beings if they did something to displease her.

Some say that Queen Mother of the West lived on a remote western mountain called Kunlun. Others claim that she lived in a castle of gold that stood next to a bejeweled lake on that mountain. The mountain was so well fortified against intruders that no human ever got past the huge wall that surrounded it. The wall itself hid a moat whose waters were so magical that anything that fell on it instantly sank—even a silk thread! A wall of fire that no living thing could penetrate also protected her domain.

Beyond all this was the Imperial Peach Orchard, whose fruit contained the juices of immortality. The orchard was under the protective custody of Queen Mother of the West. It was the peaches from this orchard that the God of Mischief—the Monkey God— devoured when he was made the orchard's guardian.

LEI SHEN AND DIAN MU
God of Thunder
Goddess of Lightning

Natural events such as thunder, lightning, and rain frightened the people of ancient times. They thought these were the signs of an angry god.

People in ancient China believed that Lei Shen was one of these angry gods. Sometimes called Lei Gong, God of Thunder, he would throw his thunderbolts at anyone who wasted food. China often suffered great famines and millions died from starvation. It is no surprise that wasting food would anger a god.

Once Lei Shen heaved his thunderbolt at a woman who was about to throw out a bowl of rice. Frightened to death, she had no chance to waste the food. Because Lei Shen had acted too quickly, the woman he struck dead, Dian Mu, was made Goddess of Lightning. Her job was to flash a mirror so that Lei Shen could see where to throw his thunderbolts. Like Lei Shen, Dian Mu had no patience with people who wasted food. Dian Mu and Lei Shen became inseparable.

While Lei Shen was the thunder-making god, he was also responsible for the actions of Dian Mu; Yu Shi, God of the Rain; and lesser gods such as the Lord of the Wind. Lei Shen was a restless god whose very bad temper was matched by his ugliness. He had batlike wings and feet with claws and a bird's beak on his blue face. He used a hammer and drum to create thunder.

HUANG DI
God of Law and Order

Huang Di, also called the Yellow Emperor, was the first spirit emperor of China. He is not to be confused with the human Qin Shi Huangdi, the first emperor of a unified China, who lived more than two thousand years ago.

Huang Di lived in heaven and ruled over all the states that would one day be called China. He devised laws and created order so that everyone on Earth could live happily in one country instead of fearfully in a collection of warring states. In effect the Yellow Emperor was China's first supreme ruler, two thousand years before his namesake. He wasn't anything like his namesake, however. The human emperor, Qin Shi Huangdi, killed people who disagreed with him. He banished his own mother, burned books, executed artists and writers, and sliced off teachers' heads after burying them neck deep in the Great Wall because he feared an educated populace. The god Huang Di—the Yellow Emperor—liked people and tried to protect them.

People believed that Huang Di had countless children, some of whom lived in heaven as gods and goddesses, and others who lived on Earth as human beings. He is said to have invented time, clocks, and calendars. Because he lived in heaven among all the bodies of the universe, he invented instruments for tracking the movement of the planets and stars. Among his many concerns was the well-being of all humankind. Huang Di developed a vast body of medical knowledge and is credited with writing the first medical textbooks.

CAI SHEN
God of Wealth

Wealth in China was not merely a matter of money—although money was an important element on the road to happiness. But a man, woman, or family who had more boys than girls, important positions, long life, and a life of general pleasure and happiness was considered wealthy.

Everyone believed that life's fortunes rested in the hands of Cai Shen, God of Wealth. There were temples dedicated to him throughout China. The Chinese—young and old, man, woman, and child—regularly visited Cai Shen's temple and prayed for wealth. Cai Shen was never without plenty of worshipers. His image could be found in the humblest homes and shops.

Cai Shen was sometimes pictured as a pleasant old man with a white beard—a happy, gentle grandfatherly type. At other times he appeared as a richly gowned, overweight man who had plenty of everything. Cai Shen was usually accompanied by a couple of attendants carrying a pot or bowl of money. Various other images on his person symbolized other aspects of wealth, such as a golden mushroom for long life and a lotus blossom for siring sons.

HONG SHEN
God of the Southern Seas

Hong Shen's family name, Hong, means "flood." He was one of many deities who was born of people's need to be protected from the ravages of water, such as the great floods that too often destroyed villages, towns, and cities.

Sailors and fishermen prayed to Hong Shen for good weather and calm seas. The unpredictable ocean swallowed more sailors and fishermen than anyone could count. Some say Hong Shen was related to Guanyin, who could hear the cry of sailors lost at sea. Sometimes he was called the Holy One.

To the people who lived on the southern coast of China, Hong Shen was not only the King of the Southern Seas, he was also the Dragon King of the Southern Seas in human form.

It was among the southern fishing communities of ancient China that today's Dragon Boat Festival originated two thousand years ago. The festival always began at the start of summer with boat races designed to honor Quynan, an ancient statesman who drowned on the fifth day of the fifth lunar month. Later the festival included prayers for rain to water the vast rice crops that grew in the south, China's one staple food that kept the entire population—north, south, east, and west—from starvation.

Hong Shen, in his human form, is often pictured with a hot sun behind his head.

MENSHEN
Gods of Peaceful Sleep

Taizong was the first emperor in a line of powerful emperors who ruled China between 618 and 906 A.C.E. Together these rulers were known as the Tang dynasty.

Emperor Taizong spent a good deal of his reign fighting off one invading Turkish army after the next on his western frontier. He had no desire for war, but he had to protect his country. Eventually Taizong defeated these invaders and made their lands part of China.

Peace came to China but not to Emperor Taizong. He could not sleep. He had nightmares of demons running around his bed and saw warriors coming for him through the door of his bedroom. The entire royal household feared that he would die in his sleep. Two of his most trusted soldiers offered to stand guard at his bedroom door, one on each side.

That night, with the two soldiers protecting him from his unseen enemies, Taizong slept without having a nightmare. As long as the guards remained at their posts, the emperor slept well. The demons and warriors of his dreams had all disappeared. Eventually the door guards were sent away and replaced with a painting of each of them. The paintings worked. No demons haunted the emperor's dreams.

By the time Taizong died in 649, his door guards had become Menshen: the "door gods," gods of peaceful sleep. Households throughout China display them and keep nightmares away.

BIBLIOGRAPHY

Chamberlain, Jonathan. *Chinese Gods*. Selangor Darul Ehsan, Malaysia: Pelanduk Publications, 1987.

Christie, Anthony. *Chinese Mythology*. London: Chancellor Press, 1996.

Duane, O. B., and N. Hutchinson. *Chinese Myths and Legends*. London: Brockhampton Press, 1998.

Lehner, Ernst. *Symbols, Signs, and Signets*. New York: Dover, 1985.

Sanders, Tao Tao Liu. *Dragons, Gods, and Spirits from Chinese Mythology*. New York: Peter Bedrick Books, 1980.

Seeger, Elizabeth. *The Pageant of Chinese History*. New York: Longmans, Green and Co., 1948.

Stepanchuk, Carol, and Charles Wong. *Mooncakes and Hungry Ghosts: Festivals of China*. San Francisco: China Books and Periodicals, 1991.

PRONUNCIATION GUIDE
The following pronunciations are based on the Mandarin language.

Mazu: mah-dzu

Wen: wehn

Jiao: jee-ou ("ou" as in *out*)

Chang: chang (rhymes with *hang*)

Qin: chin

Shi: shir

huang: hwahng

Da: daah

di: dee

Shang: shahng

Nü: knee, with puckered lips

Wa: wah

Fu: foo

Xi: she, with tip of tongue on bottom teeth

Sun: swun (the vowel sounds like the "woo" in *wood*)

Wu: oo

Kong: kung (the vowel sounds like the "ou" in *could*)

Guan: gwahn

Yin: in

Miao: meow

Zhong: jong (the "j" sounds like the "dge" in *fudge*)

Kui: kwee

Niu: nee-oh

Lang: lang (rhymes with *hang*)

Zhi: ji (the "j" sounds like the "dge" in *fudge*)

Shan: shahn

Gong: gung (the vowel sounds like the "ou" in *could*)

Wei: way

Shu: shoe

Liu: lee-oh

Bei: bay

Wang: wang (rhymes with *hang*)

Mu: moo

Kun: kwun (the vowel sounds like "woo" in *wood*)

Lun: lwun (the vowel sounds like the "woo" in *wood*)

Lei: lay

Shen: shung (rhymes with *rung*)

Dian: dee-ohn

Yu: ee, with puckered lips

Cai: tsy

Shen: shen

Hong: hung (the vowel sounds like the "ou" in *could*)

Tai: tie

zong: dzong (the vowel sounds like the "ou" in *could*)

To Barbara Walsh

This book uses the pinyin style for romanization.

The publisher would like to thank Dr. Duanduan Li, Director of Chinese Languages at Columbia University's East Asian Languages and Cultures Department, and Assistant Professor Carrie E. Reed of Middlebury College's Chinese Department, for their assistance.

Library of Congress Cataloging-in-Publication Data
Fisher, Leonard Everett.
The gods and goddesses of ancient China / Leonard Everett Fisher.
p. cm.
Includes bibliographical references.
ISBN 0-8234-1694-1
1. Gods, Chinese. 2. Goddesses, Chinese. I. Title.
BL1812.G63 F57 2003
299'.51—dc21 2002068802

LANDS of ANCIENT CHINA

RUSSIA

Note: There are two *Wei*s on this map. They sound the same, but are written in different Chinese characters.

MONGOLIA

KYRGYZSTAN   KAZAKSTAN

CHINA

TAJIKISTAN

AFGHANISTAN

PAKISTAN

TIBET

NEPAL

BHUTAN

BANGLADESH

INDIA

MYANMAR
(BURMA)

BAY OF
BENGAL